FINANCIAL INDEPENDENCE
DOESN'T HAPPEN BY ACCIDENT

FINANCIAL INDEPENDENCE

DOESN'T HAPPEN BY ACCIDENT

A GUIDE TO DEVELOPING YOUR OWN
FINANCIAL INDEPENDENCE ROADMAP

MALCOLM ETHRIDGE

CONTENTS

CONTENTS

FOREWORD

I'm so happy you're reading this book.

For 15 years I hosted "Motley Fool Money", a podcast about investing that's also syndicated to radio stations across America. Every week I would interview authors, business reporters, and experts in all areas of finance.

The first time I interviewed Malcolm Ethridge was in 2017. I already knew he was smart and credentialed, but what struck me was how methodically he approached the topics of money and investing. While I've interviewed hundreds of people, Malcolm is on the short list of financial experts I had the pleasure of having as repeat guests.

In this book, Malcolm does the same thing he did whenever I talked with him for my show or whenever he's interviewed on CNBC–he methodically presents his case in a clear, thorough, and entertaining way. This is what he does for his clients on a daily basis. And here, for you, he shares a straightforward framework for how anyone can achieve financial independence.

This is why I'm happy you're reading this. You're taking the first step towards a brighter financial future by reading the book Malcolm Ethridge was meant to write.

Chris Hill

INTRODUCTION

If your parents are a part of the Baby Boomer generation like mine - or maybe yours belong to the silent generation - you likely grew up watching them get up and go to work Monday to Friday, 9 am to 5 pm, at the same job, for decades, until one day, they turned sixty-five and retired with that coveted gold watch and fully-funded pension.

When you were a kid, you likely assumed your own life would go something like that, too.

While I was in college figuring out what the future had in store for me, I watched my mom retire from the job she'd held for 33 years, which happened to be her second job out of nursing school.

I, like many children of Baby Boomers, assumed that this was simply the normal trajectory of adult life: go to school, get "good" grades, get into a "good" college, get a "good" job, and things will work themselves out.

Little did we know, the world had different plans in store for us...

If you're a Millennial like me, you likely graduated high school or college into the Great Recession. You struggled to get a job and find your footing due to a devastated economy that saw folks with PhDs working as bartenders and baristas to make ends meet.

Over the next decade or so, you gradually got yourself on track and began to feel some semblance of adulthood and independence. Maybe you found a "good" job that allowed you to pay down your student loans, buy your first home, or give you the confidence to start a family.

Then, bam! Your world was rocked once again—this time by a global pandemic that would see many millions sidelined and out of work—some of whom never returned to the workforce at all.

For a fortunate few, the impact of the pandemic was minimal. It was simply a minor inconvenience and an opportunity to work on a craft or find a new hobby. But for others, the result may have been financial strain, which required them to burn through savings, tap into retirement accounts early, or even move in with family.

All the while, the thought lingering in the back of your mind is something like, "At this rate, I'm never going to be able to retire at 65 with my gold watch and my pension."

And you'd be right. That world does not exist anymore for those too young to be called a Baby Boomer. Even if that world did exist, the idea of working 9-to-5 until you turn sixty-five doesn't appeal to most Millennials, Gen-Z, and even Gen-X.

We don't want to do it the way Mom and Dad did it.

Thus, the phenomenon we witnessed throughout 2020 and 2021, colloquially referred to as "meme stock mania," should be seen as a rebuffing of the old model. Rather than dismissing the entire moment as simply a group of young, inexperienced retail investors looking to strike it rich by gambling in the stock market, perhaps we should consider that what was underlying that period (and continues today) was that younger people are looking to play catch up.

Young people were promised that if they went to college and worked hard, they would get a fair shot at achieving their American Dream. Yet, over 50% of Gen Xers are feeling the financial strain of caring for their adult parents while simultaneously raising their own children, 50% of Millennials still do not feel like they will be able to own a home, and only 35% of Gen-Zers say that they feel confident about their ability to retire someday.

With that in mind, it is worth considering that at least some of the people who took to the stock market using apps such as Robinhood and others during this time weren't simply looking to strike it rich overnight. It was more than that. For some, this was seen as an opportunity to close that gap—and do it much earlier than age 65.

This doesn't mean they were looking to be entirely out of the workforce by age 30, 40, or 50. Instead, they were hoping that by choosing the right stock at the right time and going all in, they would be able to put away enough cash and create enough of a cushion to create some breathing room.

Though they may not have labeled it as such, what this group was truly looking for was some semblance of financial independence.

Yet, with no clear path to financial success, many younger people feel overwhelmed and confused. They think, "I'm struggling to even earn enough money... let alone save anything for tomorrow." "Will I ever be able to buy a house and get my parents off my back?" "I'm Googling, but with so much conflicting information out there, I can't tell what to believe." "Do I really have to wait until I'm a senior citizen to live the life I want to live?"

When most people hear the term *financial independence,* they think of it as some lofty goal that's impossible to achieve. They picture the extreme case of winning a multi-million dollar lottery prize or some other sort of life-altering windfall.

For the majority of people, financial independence won't happen by accident. But the truth is, it's something that can be attained by anyone who is willing to think differently and work toward it daily.

On top of knowing what to do, achieving financial independence will require intentionality, patience, and discipline. But it *is* a pursuit that is well worth the effort.

One evening in 2018, I was driving home, down Interstate 95, from a conference somewhere in Philly, when I saw a billboard that struck me. It said, "20 years from now, the only people who will remember you stayed to work late are the people you're driving home to."

This one sentence hit me upside the head so hard I've never been able to forget it. At the time, my wife and I hadn't even gotten engaged yet, but now that I'm married, with a little one who loves nothing more than my undivided attention, the message on that billboard rings even truer.

As the billboard makes clear, our bosses, co-workers, and clients may not remember the sacrifices we make to succeed in our careers, but our families and friends will remember the times we were not there because we prioritized career success over something else. This doesn't mean that we should stop working hard altogether or feel guilty when we need to take time away from family.

However, it does mean that we can make a decision to work hard, with guardrails, *so that we can build a better long-term future for ourselves and our loved ones.* For example, since I prefer not to sacrifice weekend time with my family for work, I implemented a rule that I do not attend conferences or other professional events that take place on the weekend. While I'm very much aware that such a rule might cost me some unknowable financial opportunity, I like to think that the trade-off is very much worth it.

Working hard and making money isn't the sole purpose of life anyway. No one's goal should be to die the richest person in the nursing home. Instead, money is meant to be used as a tool to help improve our quality of life. That may include doing things with the people we love, or it may mean having the freedom to do nothing at all. But having that choice is what financial independence is all about.

The journey to financial independence is about making strategic, intentional financial decisions that build a future in which we aren't bound by the constraints of working for our next dollar. When we are financially independent, we have the ultimate freedom over our time, and can focus on fulfilling our true purpose in life—whatever that looks like for you.

Financial independence is not a fantasy, nor is it a get-rich-quick scheme. In this book, I will share some practical, actionable steps that anyone can take to build a financially independent future.

CHAPTER 1
WHAT IS FINANCIAL INDEPENDENCE?

Traditionally, we are taught that work is supposed to happen between the hours of 9:00 AM to 5:00 PM, five days per week, 50 weeks per year, for 40+ years, until age 65 or later. Then, and only then, are we allowed to think about and prioritize the people and things that matter to us most.

But younger generations are toppling this idea that work is supposed to be the most important thing in our lives. In reality, we should also be spending our younger years enjoying time together with friends and family, exploring and traveling, and dedicating our time to the causes that we care about.

If you were to ask just about any adult what the most valuable thing in life is, I bet they would almost unanimously tell you it's time. But if I were to tell you that it's possible to buy yourself more time, you'd assume I was describing the plot to a sci-fi movie starring Justin Timberlake and not a core concept of personal finance.

But that's exactly what saving and investing your way to financial independence is. It's buying yourself more time for the people and the things that really matter to you.

You're not just trying to amass a fortune on paper so you can sit back, look at the number, and feel good about yourself. You're trying to use the money or assets that you're generating as the vehicle to reach your goals.

Often, when people hear the term financial independence, they think of extreme cases such as winning a multi-million dollar lottery prize or being a billionaire with a private island and a couple of jets. But this doesn't have to be the case. For some, financial independence could be as simple as owning a home that's paid off or working for yourself.

Financial independence means that the money you make while you're asleep exceeds the expenses that you have on a monthly or annual basis. It means you've managed to get your passive income streams higher than your expenses, so you can live comfortably without relying on someone else for your paycheck. It means you're able to cover your expenses without having to worry about whether you'll have a job tomorrow or not.

You may have heard about financial independence before from influencers advocating for "silver bullet" solutions that often amount to little more than gambling or scams.

There's no silver bullet solution that will take you to financial independence overnight, but there is a proven path. I can tell you it's the proven path because of the hundreds of clients I have worked with in my day job to help identify, target, and in many cases, reach their own financial independence point.

What Financial Independence is Not

The FIRE (Financial Independence, Retire Early) Movement has gained popularity in recent years as Gen-X, Millennials, and Gen-Z seek to break the "9-to-5 until 65" mold. Many proponents of this movement live in van communities and essentially take a vow of poverty so that they can exit the workforce as quickly as possible.

But some of the most well-known influencers and gurus glamorize their FIRE lifestyles on social media while hiding that they've had to take on odd jobs and perform gig work just to stay afloat. Others romanticize their extreme frugality and preach living on just a couple of dollars each day while making tens of thousands of dollars every month through corporate partnerships and ad-supported content.

You don't have to be an extremist to reach your financial independence point.

I know many so-called financial experts will tell you that cutting your spending down to the bare minimum is the only way to go. However, pursuing financial independence doesn't mean you have to deny yourself all the things you love. It means identifying the places you really enjoy spending money, the things that spark joy, and cutting back on the rest.

For instance, I'm a marathoner. Running long distances not only helps keep me in great physical shape, but it helps me think deeply, and that brings me joy. Thus, I will never feel guilty about the amount of money I spend on a pair of quality running shoes.

But when you pursue financial independence, you don't get to have it all. I don't spend hundreds of dollars on regular shoes (or any other types of apparel really) because that doesn't bring me joy. I limit my ridiculous spending on clothes and shoes to the running category and look for sales and coupons for all other articles of clothing I might buy. To be able to spend freely on what makes me happy, I have to conscientiously decide to limit spending on items that don't actually matter to me.

But the FIRE movement doesn't make room for joyful spending. It preaches that the only way to break loose from the workforce is to cut all spending to the bare minimum. In the process, followers may gain a few extra decades of retirement, but what's the point of having all that extra time on your hands if you have to sacrifice your happiness?

If you're still not convinced, I would encourage you to chat with just one of the 30-somethings who was inspired to commit to the FIRE movement, sold all of their worldly possessions, moved into a van, retired before their 35th birthday, and five years later was miserable.

Missing out on fun with your friends and important family events just for the sake of saying you're retired in your 30s is not worth it if you don't actually get to enjoy yourself every now and then. Some FIRE followers even reported divorcing their spouses or cutting off family members if they weren't on board with their new lifestyle. But, what's the point of creating this better life for yourself if you have no one left to share it with by the time you get there?

The relentless focus on being frugal and not spending a dollar on anything is a job in itself. Can you imagine living in a van until you're 90 just for the sake of not having a job? Instead, what if you found a job you actually enjoyed or pursued income off-and-on in a series of four-year sprints?

Extremism doesn't work. People who crash diet and go to extremes to lose weight in short periods of time often find themselves in worse shape than before. And people who try to quickly gain financial independence through extreme measures often find that these lifestyles aren't sustainable.

It's my own belief that much of the industry that has been built up around the FIRE movement is not designed to help you find and reach your own path to financial independence or to set you on course to reach your own goals. It's for so-called gurus looking to sell an online course or a series of workbooks or lifestyle coaching that puts them on their own path to financial independence.

In reality, they don't care if you ever reach financial independence on your own or not. They care about whether *they* reach financial independence.

Similarly, the meme stock mania of the last several years built momentum off of FOMO, convincing many young people they could have overnight success if only they had jumped on the bandwagon with everyone else. Online communities developed herd mindsets and made others feel dumb for not joining the hype around the viral investment of the month.

This book aims to help you develop your own roadmap to financial independence, not make you feel bad about yourself because you're older than 30 and not already a multi-millionaire. My goal is not to preach to you as a shoeless FIRE guru in the woods or convince you from behind a keyboard that the hot stock of the moment will make you wealthy beyond your wildest dreams.

Instead, my goal is to help you determine where you want to go, develop a plan to get there, and then take action to get to your financial independence point. It's about helping you start where you are today by putting one foot in front of the other toward the life you want.

I'm not telling you what you *should* be nor what you *should* have. I'm telling you how to get where you want to go. There's no money shaming or unnecessary comparisons intended to make you feel like you're missing out. That's what Instagram is for.

This book will share a realistic approach to how long it takes to build financial independence from the perspective of someone who earns his living advising high-net-worth individuals on how to best save, spend, and invest their financial resources every single day. I'm not just some guy who has an opinion because he paid off his car loan a month early and made a YouTube video about it that went viral.

My goal here is not to sell you a system or a course that's going to make you an overnight success. It's to share some of the same information and concepts that I share with clients every single day. The financial independence roadmap is a tried and true process that is sustainable and delivers results, not one that will give you a temporary sugar high intended to last only a few moments.

Here, we're not going to follow the extreme, "all or nothing" approach of the FIRE movement. Instead, like working with a good personal trainer, we're going to set small goals initially and then increase the intensity of the work we're doing to reach those goals over time. The process of building financial independence will require time, hard work, and commitment, but it will win you control over your life that is lasting and sustainable.

Breaking the Mold

Most of our parents and grandparents didn't manage money for financial independence. They didn't have to—they grew up with the comfort of the "9-to-5 until you're 65" model that guaranteed them a gold watch and fully funded pension at retirement.

The financial advice they gave you growing up (and maybe even still today) was tailored to that model. Even though I've been successful in my career for over a decade, my dad still occasionally emails me listings for "safe" government jobs he thinks I should consider just in case. Securing such a job in his 30s would have been the ultimate prize to him as a Baby Boomer. However, what he doesn't realize is that I enjoy a much higher degree of autonomy and control over my life in my current career.

If we're going to pursue financial independence, we have to recognize that our older relatives' advice to seek safety in our careers, above all else, is well-meaning. But it isn't the best advice for today's world. It's like someone trying to give you driving directions today based on what the city looked like fifty years ago. The landscape has changed.

We have to shake much of the financial advice we've been handed down from older generations. We can be grateful that the advice they've given us has gotten us to where we are today while acknowledging that it won't get us where we want to go in the future. We're going to have to break the mold and do things differently.

As you begin this journey, keep in mind that your older relatives may tell you your goal isn't possible or look at you like you're crazy when you explain the decisions you're making. Don't be swayed by what Mom and Dad think you should do with your money. The rules of the game have changed over the last several decades, so it's only reasonable that we're going to have to adjust and learn to play by them.

Allow Yourself to Dream

The first step is to know where you're going. Spend some time imagining your best self and what it would mean to live life on your own terms. How do you define financial independence for yourself? What would a life that's truly yours even look like? What would it feel like? Where would you go? Who would you take with you? Who would you leave at home?

It's important to let yourself dream and envision what is possible before you do anything else. You need to know what you're working toward. After all, when the vision is clear, the decisions are easy.

This isn't the part of the exercise where you start doing the math or assigning numbers to anything. There will be plenty of time for that later. This is the part where you literally sit peacefully, meditate, and think deeply about what type of life you want for yourself just 10 years from now.

Imagine it. Think about how you would move through life if you knew there was a finite number of years you still needed to work full-time to earn a living. If you could point to a graph and say "5 years from now, or 10 years from now, I'm out of here" how would you do things differently?

If you woke up tomorrow morning and suddenly found that you had more than enough money to cover all of your expenses and have some fun as well, what would your life look like from then on? Would you still work? Would you find a different job than the one you have now? Would you travel? Would you move abroad? Would you volunteer?

Sit with those questions for a moment. Take notice of what answers begin to form and what emotions you feel in response to those answers.

If money was not a factor in your decision-making at all, how would you occupy your days?

Achieving financial independence will get you off the 9-5 treadmill and out of the habit of working for the sake of working, with only two days each week to rest and take care of yourself. But what then? When you find that you have successfully broken the mold and disproved all of the naysayers, what happens next?

Often, people will still think about this question in terms of work. That's because our society conditions us to think that what we do for work is who we are. Usually, people's first answer to this question is, "Oh, I'll go work in a role that I love but that doesn't make much money." Or "I'll work for a non-profit." Or "I'll teach." But all of these things are still jobs.

It's okay if the answer to this question is a job—it's great that you love what you do—but the point of this question is to think bigger and consider how we would really want to spend our time if money was no object and we weren't limited to a career as our only way to define success.

When we have a job, we trade time for money. For the young worker, fresh out of college with all of the energy to work hard but without much more than just a dollar to their name, trading in every available hour to earn more money might seem like a fair trade. Meanwhile, an older person nearing the end of their life might be willing to trade a few dollars for more time.

I believe that wedged somewhere between those two extremes, there is a crossover point where time becomes more important than money, but you've also accumulated enough money to have the freedom to spend that time the way you choose. However, many career-driven individuals often overlook this pivotal point once they reach it, continuing to prioritize earnings over personal fulfillment.

The key, then, is to reach this inflection point soon enough that you have the ability to trade off some of your money for more time to spend on activities that bring you meaning or enjoyment. The problem, though, that many people face is as their incomes increase over time, so too do their lifestyle expenses, limiting their ability to save the money that they could use to "buy" more time later on.

The last piece of this visualization exercise is to determine what is negotiable and what isn't. What are you willing to give up in pursuit of your financial independence goal? What are you not willing to compromise on? What level of discomfort are you willing to tolerate in exchange for financial freedom?

Once you have the vision of your ideal financially independent life, you can start to work backward and plan the strategic steps you will take to make it a reality.

CHAPTER 2
WHAT THE TRADITIONAL FINANCIAL SERVICES INDUSTRY LEAVES OUT

Once upon a time, somewhere in the 1950s and 60s, stockbrokers who focused on selling their "clients" the hot stock of the day ruled Wall Street. Whether it was shares of Disney, Pepsi, Coca-Cola, or some other blue chip company that had been around long enough to have name recognition, those who were in the know accumulated a portfolio full of these companies' shares over time. And once they got far enough down the road that it was time to file for the pension and get fitted for the gold watch, cashing out these stocks provided the money they would have to retire on.

A decade later, municipal bonds became the "it" product. The name of the game was to simply buy enough municipal bonds with high enough interest payments that the income you received from them each month would be enough to supplement your retirement income. This was seen as the safer alternative to stocks since, as long as you held those bonds until maturity, you (almost) couldn't lose your money.

Then, in the 1990s, with the increased popularity of the 401(k), mutual funds became more of a focus. The big bank-owned brokerage firms had their favorite "mutual fund of the day" that they would sell a few shares of to anyone with a social security number and a pulse. The promise was if you put enough cash into your broker's favorite mutual fund each payday, over a 20 to 30-year period, you'd have enough saved by the time you were ready to pick out the cake for your retirement party.

But in the last decade or so, the industry has slowly begun to have the awakening that what people really need is advice and guidance – not products. And the advice needs to encompass their entire financial picture, not just their investments.

Now, the financial services industry is attempting to evolve into giving people advice on how to use all of the instruments that are available to them to create an income plan for a comfortable retirement. But that is still advice intended to work for an old model.

Admittedly, my beloved financial services industry has done a terrible job for the last five, six, or seven decades of giving people advice on how to save, spend, and invest their hard-earned money, as a means to getting from point A to point B. For too long, the focus has been on selling financial products to people who may or may not even need them.

The industry is headed in the right direction, but many financial advisors are still not adapting to a world beyond the Baby Boomer's idea of pursuing a comfortable retirement. With Gen-X, Millennials, and Gen-Z redefining life beyond the "9-to-5 until you're 65" grind, limiting the scope of financial advice to this model does many people a disservice.

Where Traditional Advice Falls Short

Much of the financial advice industry is still talking to the Baby Boomers...not to you.

Regardless of the platform, the most common marketing material you see out there features two people in their 70s, sitting in Adirondack chairs or walking along the beach with no shoes on.

Most of the industry has not figured out how to communicate with people in their 30s, 40s, and 50s who are seeking financial independence - not retirement. The industry has been focused on the biggest population group with the most money, which has been the Boomers. This means that younger people are getting advice that's intended for a different generation who lived through very different job markets, economic conditions, and cultural norms.

The boomers grew up with the "9 to 5 until you're 65" model as one to aspire to. As a result, this is the language that much of the personal finance industry still communicates with to this day. Even though younger generations don't view work and retirement in this way, we still talk and teach about money as if everyone's goals are the same.

If you're seeking financial independence in your 30's, 40's, or 50's, you can't follow a plan designed to get seniors ready for retirement. Determining how to keep from outliving your savings at 65 is a much different equation to solve than figuring out how to reach financial independence when you're younger.

The financial services industry is still marketing towards younger people with the same messaging they used to target boomers when they were younger people. It's delusional of them to act as though nothing has changed over the last four to five decades.

Essentially, the industry's messaging to younger people is "Go get rich first, then call me when you're 65 and ready to retire." But the message should be, "I will come along with you on your journey and help you become rich faster than you'd be able to on your own."

Not only is the industry's marketing stuck in the past, but the approach is, too. The way financial professionals typically approach the planning process assumes your sole focus is to accumulate enough tax-deferred retirement assets to be able to retire at 65.

Another contributor to this problem is who's in charge. In the U.S., it's Congress that sets the laws regarding retirement and the tax code. And while the median age of an American citizen is 38.9 years old, the median age of a Congressperson is nearly 60 years old. In the U.S. Senate, it's closer to 70.

Thus, there is a huge generational disconnect between the people who are making the laws and the people affected by them. Our lawmakers grew up in a "9 to 5 until you're 65" world, so that's the mindset with which they legislate. The financial services industry clearly follows the direction set by our elected officials, and as a result, many of its systems are not built to help younger people achieve financial independence any sooner than the government has determined we should be allowed to.

Beware of the Wolf in Financial Advisor's Clothing

There's a scene in the movie *The Wolf of Wall Street* in which the character, played by Leonardo DiCaprio, is taken out to lunch on his first day working on Wall Street by a more experienced broker, played by Matthew McConaughey.

When Leonardo DiCaprio says he's excited to start at the firm because they have great clients, Matthew McConaughey immediately interrupts him by exclaiming, "F*** the clients." He goes on to say that the "Name of the game [is to] move the money from [the] clients' pocket into your pocket." He tells the new broker not to worry about whether his clients are making money or not, and that his goal should be to sell them a product and pocket the commission either way.

Though I'd love to believe that all of the financial services industry has moved away from this mindset, there is still too much evidence to the contrary. Even those financial professionals who truly believe, deep down, that the product they sell or the company they represent has all of the best intentions, there is still the chance that it might not be the right fit for the person it's being sold to. And it really doesn't matter what the product is—you can't get to financial independence with any one solution.

To that end, it is important to recognize that life insurance is not a financial plan. But just about everyone you meet who sells insurance for a living will insist that the solution to the problem you're facing is some sort of life insurance product.

In all fairness, this does make some sense. Because if you're a carpenter, and the only tool you have in your bag is a hammer, then every problem looks like a nail to you. Engaging with a life insurance salesperson for your financial planning needs is no different. Every problem they attempt to help you solve is going to have a life insurance solution tied to it because that's the only tool they have in the bag.

To be clear, in no way am I against owning life insurance. In fact, I own plenty of it myself. But, life insurance is traditionally purchased with the intention of providing an income stream for anyone who depends on you financially, in the event that you die unexpectedly. The proceeds from the policy pass to any named beneficiaries tax-free and, at a minimum, help to ensure they do not experience a significant drop in their standard of living.

That's it. The question should not be about how much insurance you can afford, but rather how much you actually need. There is a time and a place for life insurance—it solves an important problem. But it doesn't solve every problem.

CHAPTER 3
SO WHAT SHOULD I DO?

With so much noise out there in the world and seemingly endless streams of information coming at us from all angles, it's hard to know what the truth is. This is why finances leave most people in a constant state of frustration mixed with confusion.

Often, the information you're scrolling past and unconsciously consuming on social media is conflicting. You may watch a TikTok lauding a new crypto token that's headed to the moon, only to open Instagram and see a different influencer breaking down the 10 reasons why this new coin is a scam.

Who should you listen to for financial advice? Where should you even start? In a sea of constant information, it's hard to know which information is correct. And how do you know who truly has your best interest at heart and who is just looking to profit off of you? Does this influencer know what they're talking about, or are they just trying to sell a course? Is it really possible to to buy millions of dollars of rental real estate with absolutely no money down or is someone about to make a hefty commission off my ignorance?

It's difficult to know who to listen to or trust, so many people develop "analysis paralysis" and don't do anything. However, it is important to understand that the choice to do nothing is still a choice.

Some get into the habit of trying to "over-optimize." They're in search of the perfect solution, and they won't rest until they find it. But the pursuit of the perfect solution prevents them from taking action, too. With personal finance, most of the time, there is no 100% perfect solution.

Perfection shouldn't be the goal anyway. It's unattainable since the variables needed to make a decision are constantly changing. The moment you create a financial plan, it becomes obsolete because some variables will immediately change - you're older than you were 5 minutes ago, you just earned another $5 in the stock market, and your house went down in value. Thus, there will never be an optimal solution.

Just as plans for other parts of your life are never set in stone, nor should your financial plans be. They should constantly be adapting to life's ever-changing variables. On the journey to financial independence, we need to let go of striving for perfection. Instead, we should strive to make the most reasonable decision we can at the current moment using the data that we have available.

Develop a bias toward action. Rather than waiting for the optimal solution to present itself, try something and see what happens. Then, reconfigure your plan based on what you observe. And iterate. And iterate. This approach will get you much closer to your ultimate goal than sitting still and collecting data in perpetuity, always waiting for the perfect moment to act. Such a moment will never come.

Pursuing and attaining financial independence won't happen just because you woke up today, read this book, and made a vision board about it. It's going to require you to move with some intentionality from here on out.

For instance, if your plan is to start by saving more of your paycheck every couple of weeks, rather than simply saying you want to save more, determine what "more" actually means and then assign a value to it. Write down the goal and the steps you're going to take to get there, then give it a deadline—because a goal without a plan is only a wish.

Write down the action steps you're going to take to progressively increase your income and reduce your expenses simultaneously over time. This is not the part where you have to worry about getting the math perfectly right. Your financial independence roadmap is meant to be a working plan that will evolve over time.

Pursuing financial independence will also require you to let go of any self-limiting beliefs and see things differently. Setting a goal that's too easy to reach is almost as pointless as not setting one at all. Don't let where you've been keep you from thinking big when envisioning where you can go.

Invest in Your Financial Education

If you're insecure about money, more money will never solve that. You should instead seek to be as informed and educated about your money situation as possible.

It baffles me how many of us will spend tens of thousands of dollars to get formally educated and learn skills that will allow us to earn more over our lifetimes, yet we spend next to nothing to learn how to keep the money when we get it - thus, keeping us dependent on that job for far longer.

In his book *Rich Dad, Poor Dad*, Robert Kiyosaki shares how his "poor dad", a highly educated Ph.D. who never invested in understanding how money works, never became financially independent, though he worked hard his whole life. Meanwhile, his "rich dad," was not formally educated but invested in his financial education regularly, and became one of the island's wealthiest entrepreneurs.

Some people mistakenly believe that because they're educated in one area, this education is transferable to everything. But having a terminal degree in law, for instance, doesn't automatically mean you know anything about money. If you want to be financially free it's imperative that you invest in your financial education.

Once upon a time, in our parents' and grandparents' generation, it was your company's job to prepare you for your financial future. Nowadays, that's not the case. Companies have shifted this responsibility of preparing for one's own financial future to their employees.

But all is not lost. There's a plethora of online courses, as well as books written by reputable authors that can teach you skills such as managing your cash flow or building a solid investment real estate portfolio. Often, the cost of these types of courses is far less than the financial benefits you stand to receive in return.

One of my rules for investing is: don't invest in things you don't understand. If you can't explain to me how your investment is going to make money, you have no business investing in it. But this doesn't mean you can't or shouldn't invest in it ever. It just means you need to do some research before jumping in, or walk away and invest in something you do understand instead.

Likewise, if the so-called investment some financial influencer is explaining to you is so complicated that you can't understand how and when you might expect to see a return, then beware. Ask them to explain it in terms you can understand—and if they can't, it's likely that the person promoting the opportunity stands to gain more from you parting with your dollars than you will.

Though I don't own any cryptocurrency personally, I've been interested in it for a while. I wanted to understand whether there was actually some substance there, and I didn't want to let the fact that I didn't understand the technology be the only reason I decided to pass. I didn't want the fact that I didn't understand it to be the only reason I decided to pass.

So, I invested in a course taught online by a former investment portfolio manager. I also read a couple of books written by industry "insiders." Ultimately, I still arrived at about the same conclusion, which is that ninety-nine percent of the people who invest in cryptocurrency don't fully understand it and are only investing out of fear of missing out. But by spending a few hundred dollars to educate myself, I'm confident that I'd be able to spot a crypto scam a mile away.

If you're interested in investing in real estate, there are courses on the subject that can help you make more strategic investment decisions. Many people forgo educating themselves before investing in real estate and end up making costly mistakes, such as investing in a property that has a mortgage higher than the rental price they're able to charge.

Something I've learned by observing wealthier people is that they will invest in a course or book by a person they are considering doing business with just to test the waters and see whether the person truly knows what they're talking about. Wealthy people understand that a small investment now to prevent a major loss later is well worth the price of admission.

I recently heard a podcast interview with a CPA to the stars, who was discussing how big-name celebrities often find themselves in tax trouble simply because they didn't take the time to do any due diligence before trusting the people managing their money.

His examples included Rihanna, whose accountant famously ran off with millions of her dollars and wasn't found out until much later, and Steve Harvey, whose accountant failed to send in the checks he had been writing to the IRS for several years, leaving him with several million dollars due in back taxes, and even facing the prospect of jail time.

That's not to say that every bad actor is always weeded out by due diligence. Bernie Madoff and Sam Bankman-Fried managed to defraud some of the savviest investors with their elaborate financial frauds. But by even performing some very surface-level research (aka Google), and educating yourself on how the various financial instruments typically perform, you're at least likely to uncover the more obvious red flags and give yourself a fighting chance.

Investing in your financial education takes money, time, and effort, but when your financial freedom is at stake, it's well worth it. After all, the only thing that will cost you more than a good education is ignorance.

Make a commitment to get smarter about your money year after year. The tax code and the laws that govern our money are constantly changing. That means you need to be in the habit of checking in every now and then to stay current and learn about any new changes.

Adopting the Right Mindset

Your pursuit of financial independence should take some sacrifice and make you a little bit uncomfortable. Any sort of growth or self-improvement always does.

Maybe you're afraid of pursuing financial independence because you come from a household where there was never enough to go around. And now that you have a career of your own and a few dollars in the bank, you're afraid of rocking the boat. But, beware. The "9-to-5 until 65" system preys on that scarcity mindset that we were brought up with and uses it to keep us in check. It keeps us from ever questioning authority or coloring outside of the lines.

You're going to have to break free from that scarcity mindset in order to achieve financial independence. You'll also need to learn how to ignore and override that little voice in the back of your head that tells you you're crazy and that you can't do it. There's the voice that tells you that the life I'm describing to you doesn't actually exist for people like you. You'll just have to take my word for it and get to work anyway.

There's a saying that faith is not being able to see the whole staircase but taking the first step anyway. That's what the path to financial independence will require of you. You can't see the entire fully built investment portfolio in all of its glory just yet. But you will keep on adding, brick by brick until you get there.

Understand that achieving your goal will take some time. When making a decision that will impact your financial independence plan, ask whether this decision will get you incrementally closer to that goal, not whether it will get you completely there in one move.

Embrace the Power of Passive Income

The problem with the American educational system as it stands today is that you almost always become what you study. If you study accounting, you become an accountant. If you study medicine, you become a physician. But that education teaches you how to become a good employee and earn a good income, not how to become financially independent.

In fact, it's likely that the more successful you become in your respective field, the more dependent you become on your employer to keep your life going. Now you're clinging to the job for dear life and terrified of what life would look like without it.

We are taught that working hard, putting in the hours, paying our dues, and climbing our way up the ladder are the only ways to earn a decent living in this country. But in fact, the working class trade hours for dollars, while the super-rich trade ideas for dollars.

The working class believe that the only way to become rich is to put in more hours, while the super-rich understand that we only have 24 hours in a day, which means our ability to grow our wealth by putting in more hours is finite. Instead, we need to seek out ways of making income that are not directly correlated with how much time we work. Thus, we must embrace the power of passive income.

In my experience, it is nearly impossible to reach financial independence by being a diligent saver alone. By the time a person reaches their mid-sixties, if they have been a high earner most of that time, saved and invested regularly over a 30+ year career, and avoided the temptation to keep up with the Joneses, it is possible to amass a nest egg of somewhere between $2.5-3 million, depending on market performance and timing.

But keep in mind that at 65, you're saving for a shorter time horizon than if you were to jump off the 9-to-5 treadmill in your 30's, 40's, or 50's. Thus, a younger person might need to save considerably more to feel financially secure. But to get beyond that $2.5-3 million figure, your two options are to either invest in real estate and allow it to appreciate over a long period of time, or to be closely attached to a business that creates significant value over time. The prudent approach is a mix of both.

CHAPTER 4

ENOUGH IS ENOUGH

If you're lucky, there comes a point in your journey where the next dollar you earn is less additive to your life overall and has a diminishing return. This is the point where it makes sense to begin investing in income-generating assets that will help get you off the treadmill.

A now infamous 2010 study said that money increases happiness up to a point—after about $75,000 a year, more money won't make you any happier. Over the last decade, several competing studies have emerged stating different numbers... Some say it's actually $100,000, some say $200,000, and some even say they need as much as $500,000...

Whatever the number truly is, at the heart of these studies is the idea that more money can only make you happier up to a certain point. Having a nice house is great, but do you need the biggest, nicest house on the block to live comfortably? Probably not. Driving a nice car is great, but considering our cars spend 95%

of their lives sitting in park, do you need the nicest car Mercedes manufactures? Probably not.

As you earn more money, you gain greater control over your life. You also have more free time, since you're able to outsource things you don't enjoy doing, and you're also able to pay for convenience. But once you're at a level where you can comfortably afford the things that bring you the most joy, more money likely won't add much to your overall happiness. Believe it or not, several people have even expressed to me that they see it as a burden having to figure out what to do with the excess.

Take some time to reflect on your own "enough" point. I can't define it for you. Everyone has different needs and wants. But once you've discovered where your "enough" point is, stick to it. Remember, enough is enough.

With any excess income you receive, that's above and beyond your "enough" point, rather than buying that next thing that won't add much value to your life anyway, you can invest those dollars into income-generating assets that will help you get off the "9-to-5 until 65" treadmill earlier. When you know your "enough" point, it's easier to avoid the temptation of conspicuous consumption and put your money to work instead. After all, true happiness comes when we learn to want the things we already have.

I'm aware that I could go out and buy the nicest car that Mercedes manufactures (which is an AMG G63 by the way) tomorrow morning if I wanted it. And I'm sure they would gladly sell it to me. Instead, I drive a Jeep, which has all of the bells and whistles I could ever want in a car. So at the moment, there's no reason for me to go out and get that G-Wagon.

I reserve the right to change my tune once I've reached my own financial independence point. But a nicer car won't make me happier than being financially independent will. Not by a long shot.

Don't Go Broke Trying to Not Look Broke

I will go out on a limb and assume that if you are reading this book, and you've made it this far without using these pages for kindling in a bonfire, you are not the type to carry around excessive credit card balances in the name of "keeping up." But just in case someone needed to hear it today, I will remind you that spending money you do not actually have in order to impress people you do not actually know will inevitably keep you on the "9-to-5 until 65" treadmill.

Being in a constant cycle of using this month's paycheck to pay for last month's purchases is a dangerous habit to build. But if we're not careful, that is exactly what social media breeds. We are constantly being bombarded with images of other people with seemingly better clothes than we have, taking better vacations than we are, and eating at better restaurants than we do.

We convince ourselves that we need to level up. We think that people care what we wear, where we go, and what we eat. But in reality, no one cares. I mean that literally and with the utmost sincerity. Aside from your close family, no one on social media cares what you're doing. We're all too busy looking at *ourselves* to even notice anyone else.

Remember that time you bought that pair of jeans that were $500, took that perfect picture of yourself wearing them, posted it, and then took it down the next day because it only got 12 likes? That's because the average post on social media only gets about 8 seconds of attention. Then, it's on to the next one.

And even if, for the sake of argument, it got 1,200 likes instead, how many people actually "liked" the jeans, and how many simply tapped the screen because that's what our minds are now programmed to do? In reality, most people are spending their time on social media looking at how many people liked *their* stuff, not actually looking at *your* stuff.

It's important to avoid the temptation to level up your lifestyle with each and every pay increase - otherwise known as "lifestyle creep." Lifestyle creep is like Newton's First Law. Once it's in motion, it tends to stay in motion. That can be especially dangerous because there's always something else to buy.

Every day, savvy brand managers invent new trends for us to spend our hard-earned money, in an attempt to keep up with the lifestyles of the rich and famous. These companies and their marketing departments are adept at making us feel like we actually *need* that new item just to keep up. But just when you think you've "kept up" - you finally pull out your card and order those boots that have been following you around the internet for weeks - they raise the bar on you.

To be clear, my point is not that you shouldn't reward yourself whenever you achieve a big milestone or receive a big pay increase. By all means, treat yourself. But, beware. Your boss probably wants you to fall into the trap of increasing your living expenses along with your income. That's how they keep you on the hook, coming back for more. If you know you need this job to afford your lifestyle, you're willing to put up with a lot more than someone who doesn't.

Imagine for a moment that you were to walk into work tomorrow for your weekly sit-down with your manager. And for the last few weeks, you've been dreading seeing this particular meeting on your calendar. Maybe you've been going back and forth for a while now over an assignment that just didn't sit right with you. And up to this point, you haven't quite been able to find your voice to express your displeasure, for fear that it might result in you being fired.

But this morning, that same weekly check-in went a little differently. At the end of this one, you closed your laptop, grabbed your phone, backed your chair away from the conference room table, looked your manager directly in the eyes, and simply said "This assignment makes me uncomfortable, and I'm not going to do it." How empowered would you feel as you walked back to your office?

The scenario I just described - however fictional - is precisely what happens when you know you have what I'll (somewhat) politely refer to here as F.U. Money. People typically think you have to be as wealthy as Warren Buffet or Elon Musk to have F.U. Money. But that's not actually the case.

In the scenario I'm describing, F.U. Money doesn't mean you have so much saved up that you can stick it to society and do whatever you want without consequence. But it does mean having enough control over your own life that you get to call the shots in just about every aspect of it.

In reality, F.U. Money could just mean that you have enough in cash and investments to last you a couple of years if you lost your income and it took you that long to find another one. Or maybe it means you own a couple of apartment buildings that pay you enough in rental income to cover your expenses each month, and would allow you to exit the workforce at the drop of a hat if you needed to. Whatever your version of it is, at its core, having F.U. Money allows you to move through life a little differently.

Your Assets Feed You, and Your Liabilities Eat You

I will share my complete views on debt later on, in a different section of this book. But for now, I will just point out that as you add liabilities to the equation, you also add more time to how long it will take you to reach your financial independence point. In some instances, taking on additional debt today will allow you to reach that point sooner than you could without it.

However, if you find yourself accumulating debt just to keep up with your friends and neighbors, then perhaps it is time to cut up the credit cards.

In Ramit Sethi's book *I Will Teach You To Be Rich*, he makes the observation that if you look at a group of four friends, a lot of times, they're all dressed the same way, eating the same things, and doing the same activities when they hang out... But it's very unlikely that all four of those friends are in the same financial position. This would mean that at least one friend in the group is out-spending their actual earnings, trying not to stick out from the group.

In this instance, it helps to just be honest with yourself and those around you. If you have found that you're repeatedly overspending in an attempt to keep up with your friends, it's important to understand that everything is not for everyone. If financial independence is truly the goal you've set for yourself, then being intentional about getting your spending under control is not negotiable.

This doesn't mean you have to deprive yourself of everything you've ever loved. But it does mean you can't afford to do it all. So, pick your spots.

If your friend group has made it a weekly tradition to meet up for Sunday brunch at a nice restaurant, and you look forward to this quality time every week, by all means, enjoy those mimosas. But what that may also mean is when your friends decide to rent a beach house for a week or travel to Europe on a whim, you choose to sit it out and have a staycation at home instead.

Or, if international travel is the thing in life that brings you the most joy, maybe you decide to skip the weekly brunch unless it's a special occasion and someone is celebrating. Everything is a tradeoff. And since you can't have it all, it's important to evaluate which activities matter to you the most, and which ones are simply nice to have.

Just Because They Approved You for It Doesn't Mean You Can Afford It

By constantly trying to have it all, you are almost certain to stay stuck on the "9-to-5 until 65" treadmill. Outside of social spending, another way people get into trouble, spending more than they bring home, is by letting their emotions decide when they go to make big purchases.

For instance, how often have you told yourself the exact amount you were willing to spend on a new car, well before you ever got to the dealership, only to walk out of there hours later with a car payment that is 10, 20, or even 50% more than what you initially budgeted for? Many people will justify this sort of blunder to themselves by saying "If I couldn't afford it, the bank wouldn't have approved me for it."

Personally, I've heard it several times. But it is complete and utter nonsense. The bank is not your kindhearted grandmother who just wants you to be happy. The bank's only goal in this equation is to make money. They're thinking, "What is the maximum amount of money we can put in this person's hand and charge them interest on that will allow them the highest probability of being able to pay it back over the next 72 months?"

Thankfully, this is one lesson I never had to learn the hard way. When I bought my first house at 19 (it's a long story), throughout the entire process, my mom reminded me every chance she got that I could only afford half as much house as the bank said I could buy. And she was right. Years later, after the housing market had crashed and I became a landlord against my will, I was only able to ride out the storm because I had a mortgage payment that was low enough for me to cover it out of my own pocket during the months when I didn't have a tenant.

But had I let my emotions make the decision for me, I'm fairly certain that the bank would have eventually taken the house in foreclosure, and this book would have been written from the twin bed in my childhood bedroom, rather than from my home office. But not everyone has someone in their life to beat them over the head with advice the way my mom did me.

In fact, back when I worked in the car business, it was frequently the friend or relative of the person purchasing the car who would reinforce this misguided belief about the bank's benevolence. They'd turn to their trusted confidant and say "I came in wanting to keep it under $400." And without fail, the person next to them would say, "Well, the bank wouldn't have approved you for it if they didn't think you couldn't afford it."

That always made the hair on the back of my neck stand up. I would always think to myself "You had one job!"

This type of emotional decision-making doesn't lead to financial independence. Instead, it leads to more time being added to your sentence.

Rather than breaking your promise to yourself and overspending, you're presented with two other choices. You can either be relentless about getting a good deal by negotiating with that car dealer as if your financial freedom depends on it, or you can choose to fall in love with a less expensive car.

CHAPTER 5

REACHING YOUR "FINANCIAL INDEPENDENCE CROSSOVER POINT"

In her book, *Your Money or Your Life*, Vicki Robin defines the financial independence crossover point as the place on a graph where the X and Y axes meet - with one representing the amount you receive each month from all passive income sources, and the other representing your monthly expenses.

Getting to this crossover point is paramount for anyone pursuing financial independence. Proponents of the FIRE movement will typically recommend that you become fanatical about cutting your expenses to the bare minimum, and rely on canned soup and ramen noodles for sustenance for the rest of your life.

What's misguided about this approach, though, is that there is a limit to how much you can cut from the expense column. Even if you somehow managed to get your monthly expenses down to zero, there is still a limit. However, there is no such limit to how much you can increase your income.

This is why it's so important to identify your "enough" point and be disciplined about staying there once you reach it. From that point on, any additional income you manage to bring in can be put toward savings or investments, getting you closer and closer to that coveted crossover point.

Pay Yourself First

We are all taught from a young age that anyone who does not pay their bills in full and on time each month is irresponsible, lazy, or otherwise bad. By the time a person reaches young adulthood, they have essentially learned that rule #1 of managing your personal finances is to pay every bill on time, no matter what.

As cliché as it can sometimes sound, the importance of paying yourself supersedes paying anyone else. This is especially true for anyone who chooses to pursue financial independence. It's an important habit to build. And one that will serve you well for the remainder of your life.

The federal government seems to understand this concept better than anyone else, considering withholding income taxes from employee paychecks wasn't always the standard playbook. Prior to the 1940s, Americans were permitted to make a lump sum income tax payment at the end of each year. But this often resulted in cash flow problems for the government.

Since tax collection is the main source of revenue for the federal government, by opting to collect taxes directly from paychecks, the government essentially pays itself first, which ensures a steadier stream of revenue throughout the year, making it easier to manage the country's finances. Withholding also helps ensure that workers make income tax payments on time each year. This method has worked well for the Department of Treasury since 1943, so why not apply the idea to our personal lives as well?

The IRS makes taking this approach easy by offering a tax deduction for each dollar saved into workplace retirement accounts up until a certain amount. This means that while you are reducing your taxable income dollar-for-dollar by fully funding your retirement account annually (up to the limits determined by your household income), you can simultaneously manage to pay *yourself* prior to paying any taxes or expenses.

Although it's important to save for retirement—and the tax benefits sure don't hurt—for anyone pursuing financial independence, it is also essential to put money away in a manner that will allow you to access it prior to age 59½ without paying early withdrawal penalties. This can include a traditional savings account, certificates of deposit, a money market fund, or even a regular brokerage account. Your decided method depends on your timeline for needing those funds and your personal tolerance for market risk.

But saving money doesn't just happen. Many people make the mistake of putting it off and make excuses like "I'll start saving next month after I buy this one thing." Others try to save based on whatever money is left at the end of the month only to discover that there isn't any money left over.

One way to avoid this outcome is to automate saving using direct deposit. Rather than relying on your own discipline to manually save money *after* you receive your paycheck, direct deposit enables you to set aside a portion of your income automatically. By designating a portion of your direct deposit to savings, you can prioritize your financial goals and build your savings effortlessly.

This is a "set it and forget it" approach that allows you to be hands-off. Don't even allow yourself the opportunity to give in to the temptation to skip a month because you want to use the money for something else. Also, don't set yourself up to be at the mercy of you remembering to make a transfer each month. The moment you miss one, you're likely to stop doing it altogether.

This strategy takes the guesswork out of your cash flow from month to month and allows for guilt-free spending. Once you've established your savings goals and set up your direct deposits, you can rest easier knowing that that trip you just booked, or those shoes that have been sitting in your shopping cart for a month, won't break the bank. You now have my permission to click the "buy" button.

Another way to level up your savings is to convert paid bills into opportunities to increase savings. Every time you pay off a debt, cancel a recurring subscription, get a raise at work, or otherwise "find" some extra cash, divert some of that windfall to your savings before you've even had a chance to think about how you'll spend it. Since it's "new" money, you likely won't even notice that it's gone.

The Skills You Already Have are Worth Something

When I say increase your income, many people will assume this means increasing your salary by getting an additional degree or certification. But realistically, anyone reading this likely already has enough on-the-job experience to increase their income without going back to school and incurring more debt.

Another misnomer is that the only way to increase your income is to be an entrepreneur. Unfortunately, social media has popularized the idea that it is shameful to have a 9 to 5 job, and that you'll never be able to achieve financial independence working for someone else. This sentiment has foolishly driven some people to self-employment who have no business being their own boss. If you work better in a more structured environment, starting your own business is not likely to yield the results you want.

In reality, it is simply a matter of preference. And in many cases, it doesn't have to be an either-or proposition. I believe that the best way to reach your financial independence point is through a combination of both - working your salaried job Monday through Friday, 9-to-5, and then clocking in as a consultant or contractor from 5-to-9 and on weekends.

You can increase your income by leveraging the skills you already have to perform services inside your wheelhouse. For instance, a schoolteacher who works 9:00 am to 3:00 pm, Monday through Friday, can create an online group tutoring program from 4:00 pm to 7:00 pm, working with students from all over. Or, a physician in a private practice could also serve as an expert witness at a few trials each month, whenever there is a need for someone with medical expertise. Or, a software engineer can use their programming skills on nights and weekends, to help non-technical founders create the minimum viable product they'll use to raise funding for their startup.

The opportunities are endless as long as you're willing to be creative. You likely have skills and expertise that are not all that impressive to you, but others are willing to pay you for them, as long as you put yourself out there.

For more than two decades, Jay Leno hosted The Tonight Show on NBC. Without fail, every Monday to Friday, there was Jay's face at 11:30 PM Eastern, ready to deliver his signature monologue. At the show's height, he earned an estimated $30 million for just one season. Yet, throughout his tenure as the show's host, Leno still went out and performed as a stand-up comic each and every weekend, because he believed it was important to have a secondary income stream that he controlled.

Similarly, former Seattle Seahawks running back, Marshawn Lynch, managed to play 12 full seasons in the National Football League without spending any of the $60 million in-game checks he earned throughout his career. This is because he recognized that he could, instead, live off of the money he earned through endorsement deals with big-name brands while investing the money he earned every Sunday as a pro athlete.

In *Rich Dad Poor Dad*, Robert Kiyosaki, tells a story about how at nine years old, he and his best friend came up with a scheme where they repurposed comic books that were given to them for free into a comic book library. They charged 10 cents for admission from each kid who entered and paid an older sibling to work as their librarian and bookkeeper after school. When it was all said and done, these nine-year-old boys managed to earn about $4 per week after expenses. And this was in the 1950s. I say again, all it really takes is a little creativity.

Put that Excess Cash to Work

Now that your synapses are firing and you're dreaming of all the ways in which you can generate additional income using the skills you already have, it is also a good idea to determine what you will do with that money. I will discuss how to build an investment portfolio from scratch in a later chapter. But for now, I want you to think about what interests you as an investor.

You might immediately presume that the only way to create passive income is by owning a portfolio of rental real estate. While this is certainly one of the more popular means of getting to the crossover point, it is far from the only option. Passive income can also come from investments in dividend-paying stocks, royalties from intellectual property, peer-to-peer lending, operating an online store, buying into a franchise business, etc. The opportunities are literally endless.

The only thing that matters is that you find ways to generate income that require next to no effort on your part. Passive income is only passive if it can be generated on your behalf, while you are asleep, at the beach, or otherwise unreachable. Think about these income-producing assets as your employees. They go out and work for you each day, and bring you back more dollars, irrespective of how you spend *your* time that day.

When you begin your financial independence journey, you may not have the additional income available to invest in developing passive income sources just yet. In this instance, the single most important thing to focus on is increasing your salary. One way to do that is to invest in *yourself* and level up your skill set. This is especially true when you are younger, and the extra dollars you can command by having that additional skill can compound for a couple of decades or more.

Another skill that will serve you well throughout your journey to reaching financial independence is salary negotiation. At any point in your career, it is a good use of money to enroll in an online course that will teach you how to negotiate your salary. While it may be impossible to quantify the compounding effects this will have on your lifetime earnings, I am confident you will make your investment back tenfold the very first time you use what you learn.

Since our work culture teaches us that climbing the ladder and chasing status is what matters most, many of us have to learn how to invest in our own happiness. Think about it: when's the last time you spent money on something simply because it made you happy? There will always be another ladder to climb, another promotion to chase, and another fancy title to aspire to. But what will happen to us once we've reached our financial independence point, only to realize we've neglected to cultivate any interests, hobbies, or passions worth getting off the treadmill to pursue?

CHAPTER 6

IRON SHARPENS IRON, EAGLES SOAR WITH EAGLES

How often in your life have you been told that it is tacky, or just plain rude, to talk about money? Chances are you only had to be taught that lesson once or twice as a kid for it to stick. But where did that idea even come from? Who was this mysterious being that convinced us all that by talking openly about money, it would make us seem classless, or maybe even poor?

Or do we instead believe it will help us to fit in better with those who have more than we do if we leave the money talk at home? If that is the case, allow me to burst your bubble.

In my day job, I have spent plenty of time around ultra-high-net-worth individuals, and I can tell you firsthand that they absolutely LOVE to talk about money. In some cases, it's the only thing they want to talk about.

These conversations tend to range from super mundane, to highly technical. This could look like, "I just got a quote to install a new pool in my backyard. Is this a reasonable amount to pay, or should I use a different company?" or "I'm deciding how to approach saving for my kid's college. What strategy worked for you?"

It is very common for the super-rich to get together and share ideas and resources. They have gatherings at each other's homes, plan private retreats, and hold exclusive investor events, all designed to help keep each other abreast of anything that will affect their money going forward. The goal of these get-togethers is not to brag, but to leverage the wisdom of crowds and help each other stay in the know.

It has been my experience that it's those who are in a much stronger financial position who have the most to share and are the most willing to share it. In fact, at any given stage in my life or career, it has been someone who was *clearly* much further along in their financial journey than I, who has impacted me the most - either by being completely candid about their own successes and failures with money, or by connecting me with valuable resources.

Either way, it's by being willing to approach these people and ask, that I have been able to leverage someone else's learned experience and sidestep some of the mistakes I would have otherwise made myself. But this requires us to let go of our fears. Whether you're concerned that it's rude, or that you will look silly by admitting what you don't know, either way, your fear of standing out cannot be stronger than your desire for financial independence.

In addition to seeking out the wisdom of those who are further along than you are, it is also important to find your tribe—friends in a similar financial position as you who also view money similarly to you. When you have a trusted group of friends with whom you can have open dialogue and learn from each other, you will also have someone to act as an accountability partner and help make sure you are staying on track to reach your goal of financial independence.

Simply identify the 3 or 4 people who you believe share your desire for financial independence and are equally committed to it. The group should make a commitment to check in with each other regularly to hold each other accountable when needed, *and* to celebrate each other's wins. Share ideas and best practices with each other. Take online courses and read books together. Use each other as a sounding board for any big changes you are considering.

Corporate CEOs often talk in private about the fact that the higher they go in their careers, the smaller their friend circle gets. This is because the pool of people who can relate to them and the journey they are on is constantly shrinking. However, in this instance, there isn't just one top spot. There is room for many on the road to financial independence. By pushing your own tribe to achieve their financial goals as you pursue your own, you help to ensure that your circle of friends won't have to change much once you finally get where you're going.

....

The Family that Discusses Money Together
Stays Together

....

I grew up in a household where one parent was a relentless saver who refused to spend money on anything unless it was absolutely necessary, and the other parent believed that money was meant to be spent. Over the years, I've come to realize that I took a page out of both books.

Although my parents had very different beliefs about money and its ultimate purpose, one thing they had in common was a willingness to talk openly and honestly about it. Granted, the conversations tended to revolve more around why it was that I couldn't have something that I was begging them to buy, but by the time I was in second grade, I had a solid understanding of how cash flow worked, how to make a budget, and the importance of a rainy day fund.

Talking openly about money with your kids prepares them for a future where their financial decisions are 100% their own. Helping them understand the tradeoffs you are making when you tell them "no" helps them understand why they can't have it all. Conversely, explaining the *why* behind your decision to say "yes" helps them understand the importance of rewarding yourself for a job well done.

I know a handful of estate attorneys, family office managers, and business managers who all work closely with the super-rich. One of the things we discuss frequently is the disconnect that exists between older relatives who helped to create the family's wealth and the next couple of generations below them who stand to inherit that wealth. There are plenty of statistics highlighting the fact that assets typically get depleted in just one intergenerational transfer. But the question that remains is, "Why?"

The main culprit is usually the lack of preparation that the next generations receive from the first generation, coupled with the expectation that once they reach a certain age, they should be able to simply figure it out. Generation 1 typically prefers to meet with their estate attorneys and accountants to ensure they've done everything imaginable to help future generations avoid taxes and probate. In essence, they do a great job of preparing the assets for their heirs, yet they fail to ever prepare the heirs for the assets.

This phenomenon isn't exclusive to the super-rich. That's just what gets the majority of media coverage since the dollars at stake are much larger and make for better headlines. But even a couple who has managed to accumulate $1 or $2 million over a lifetime, who has not communicated any of their wishes or transferred their knowledge to the next generation, is at risk of seeing all of that hard work eroded in less than eighteen months, as that is the average time it takes for 82% of inheritors to deplete an inheritance.

Money Alignment with Your Life Partner

A 2021 survey found that 73% of married (or cohabitating) American couples say that financial decisions are a source of tension in their relationship. Yet, I would venture to guess that almost none of them bothered to have a single meaningful conversation about their beliefs and values relating to money prior to moving in together.

There are countless stories out there about people who waited until after they were already married to ask their spouse about their finances - only to find out they were hundreds of thousands of dollars in debt and behind on their payments. To be fair, I do not believe that having debt should disqualify a person from the dating pool. However, I do believe that a person who is very much allergic to debt and takes great pains to pay it off as soon as it occurs would likely have second thoughts if they were to receive full disclosure from a potential partner whose credit cards were in arrears.

While it's not the best opening line on a first date to inquire about the other person's credit score and what percentage of their income they save each month, it is a good idea to introduce the conversation as early in the dating stage as possible. That way, before you've invested too much of yourself into the relationship and decided they're "the one," you and your potential partner would have had enough time to evaluate each other's financial goals and whether they align with your own.

As unromantic as it might be to say out loud, one of the biggest advantages of marriage is that two people get to combine their incomes while aiming toward the same set of goals. And assuming those two people are in alignment with each other about what those goals are, it would presumably take them less time to reach them. Yet, some couples choose to manage their finances completely separately, with each partner spending and saving however they please. I see this as a missed opportunity.

Apparently, the U.S. Government agrees with me, considering the tax code is very punitive toward married couples who file their taxes separately. In fact, a single person with the exact same income and deductions as a married person who files separately will likely end up paying less in taxes. While there are valid reasons for choosing to file separately as a married couple, such as one spouse owing a large amount in back taxes, it is important to understand what tradeoffs you are making, and how much longer it will take you to reach your goal of financial independence.

Engaging with Experts

Outside of your peers, family, and romantic partner, it can also be helpful to seek out the wisdom of financial experts. By experts, I mean those who have spent extensive time studying their respective industries, received advanced degrees and certifications, and spent years honing their craft. I do not use the term expert to describe anyone who is presumed to be worth listening to simply because they have a high follower count and make compelling online content.

True experts have likely helped hundreds or thousands of people in your shoes make a decision that you will only make once or twice in your lifetime. They've honed the ability to sift through oceans of information, distill it down to the key details, and then provide a summary of the best path forward. These professional advice givers can be valuable resources as you pursue financial independence.

Professional help doesn't have to come in the form of one-to-one interactions. Experts such as financial advisors, accountants, and attorneys are generally happy to get behind a microphone, in front of a camera, or step on a stage to share their respective points of view in a one-to-many format. Attending such events or consuming their content can be a great, low-stakes way to engage with them initially and determine whether you like their approach and methodology. Depending on how accessible your preferred expert is, you may even be able to invite them to spend some time with you and the tribe you've formed, answering questions and providing advice in a small group setting.

As you pursue financial independence, you are likely to encounter situations where your friends and family who are not on a similar journey are not able to provide much guidance. Having a trusted group of experts on your side is crucial when you need a sounding board or a second opinion. In the Internet era, many people turn to Google as the singular source of truth. However, while Google is a great place to start your search, it should not be seen as the be-all-end-all.

In addition to the ads hiding behind every other click, there is usually good, quality, factual information interspersed within your search results. The real challenge is finding the post or clip that speaks to the nuance of your own personal situation. It's one thing to have the definition of a term or concept and another to understand how to apply it.

CHAPTER 7

DEVELOP WEALTHY HABITS

If you want to become wealthy, develop wealthy habits. It's as simple as that. Often, people mistakenly assume that they will have to wait until after they're ready to purchase their first yacht to employ tactics commonly used by the wealthy.

However, you can certainly apply some of the same habits that the super-rich use to grow and protect their wealth, but at your own income level. In fact, adopting some of these same habits today will help you to join the ranks of the super-rich sooner.

When I come across a video online of one of my favorite professional athletes training, my first thought isn't, "Well, that's good for him, but I'm not there yet." My first instinct is to figure out how I can adapt the moves they're doing to my current fitness level using the equipment I already have.

If you observe what someone with $10 million is doing, instead of thinking, "Oh, I'll make sure to do that if I'm ever a millionaire," you can figure out how to apply the concept to your own life at a different scale. This will allow you to reach your financial independence point sooner, rather than trying to play "catch up" once you're already there.

Use Other People's Money

You've likely been told by your parents that debt is evil and should be avoided at all costs. However, the super-rich view debt differently. In fact, they don't even refer to it as debt. They call it leverage, and see it as a tool that can be used to enable the purchase of an asset without having to deplete their entire cash position.

The concept of leverage allows you to take the cash you would have spent on acquiring the big ticket item and instead invest it into something that will generate (presumably) more income than you are required to pay in interest to service that debt. Proper use of leverage allows your passive investments to reach cash flow positivity and gets you to your crossover point sooner.

Whether debt or leverage, no matter what you choose to call it, when used responsibly, it can allow us far more purchasing power and makes it easier to acquire appreciable assets sooner than we would be able to using cash alone.

Consider that in 2014, former Microsoft CEO, Steve Ballmer, was able to purchase the Los Angeles Clippers basketball team for $2 billion without tapping into his personal savings at all. That's because of a lesser-known strategy of the super-rich called a securities-backed line of credit (SBLOC). In short, an SBLOC allows a person to borrow against the value of their investment portfolio, the exact same way you would borrow against the equity in your home using a home equity line of credit (HELOC).

In Ballmer's case, where the lion's share of his net worth is (famously) tied to his stake in Microsoft, the use of his SBLOC allowed him the liquidity to make the highest bid by a wide margin, securing him the rights to the team, while leaving his Microsoft shares entirely intact.

Today, the Clippers franchise is worth an estimated $4.65 billion, and Ballmer still owns about 333 million shares of Microsoft stock. His stake, which he amassed over his 34-year career at Microsoft, is reportedly worth approximately $130 billion, making him the 6th richest person in the world.

To be fair, had Steve Ballmer sold enough shares to generate the cash to purchase the team outright, he'd still be one of the wealthiest people alive. However, considering his 4% stake in Microsoft gained more than $42 billion in value just in 2023 alone, he certainly would have paid one massive opportunity cost. And that's to say, nothing of the 9-figure tax break he received in the 5 years after purchasing the team.

One of the favorite strategies of the super-rich is to buy appreciable assets, borrow against them when they need access to cash, and then pass along those assets to the next generation once they die - avoiding taxes all along the way. That's because there is a provision in the tax code that allows for an heir to start their cost basis over from scratch on the date they inherit the asset instead of assuming the original owner's basis. Thus, this strategy is often affectionately referred to as "buy, borrow, and die" among the super-rich.

Know the Difference Between Productive and Unproductive Debts

Rather than shying away from debt altogether, we should instead understand that there is such a thing as both productive and unproductive debt. Simply put, productive debt is any debt that allows you to get closer to your financial independence point. For example, taking out a loan to buy a new car is productive because doing so allows you to go out and earn an income.

People often think of car loans as "bad debt" because cars are an asset that rapidly depreciates over short periods of time. But taking out an auto loan is productive if it allows you to get to work faster, pick up your kids from school, and generally live life more efficiently.

In a normal interest rate environment, it can be advantageous to use the bank's money even if you have the cash to purchase the entire vehicle outright - especially when buying new. New car dealers often offer rates as low as 2.9%, 1.9%, or even 0.0% to entice you to come in and take the car home today. At that rate - which is lower than inflation is likely to be any time soon - it becomes a no-brainer to use the bank's money and keep your own.

Unproductive debts are usually unsecured debts that aren't tied to an asset, such as credit cards and personal loans. These loans eat away at your future income and are likely being used to consume *things* rather than to cover necessities.

It is also unproductive to use a HELOC to consolidate credit card debts or consume more things. Although it is tied to an asset, if the HELOC is not used to improve the home (which increases its value) or invest in other assets, then taking on this debt is not going to get you any closer to your financial independence point.

Another popular idea of a "bad loan" is student loans. I consider this a widely agreed-upon fiction. To my mind, they allow you to receive an advanced education for the sole purpose of increasing your earning power over the remainder of your life. If earning that degree allowed you to command a higher salary than you would have without it, it's productive debt.

Think about how different your life would be if you hadn't gone to school... What would your life be like today had you not taken out the loan(s) and gotten that advanced education? What kind of home would you be living in? And in what neighborhood? What would your social circle look like? What would your kids' social circle(s) look like? What kind of car would you drive? Would you have to take on a second job just to make ends meet?

It's impossible to know just how much this one decision has impacted your life for the better, but we can certainly assume with a high degree of confidence that you are better off for it. Student loans are simply an investment into your future, and t in most cases, getting a loan to get a college degree will bring you closer to achieving financial independence than not having it would.

Taking on debt to start a business is also productive. Let's say you've crunched the numbers on launching a new venture from scratch, and the cost of doing so is $500,000. If you put up the $500,000 in cash, those assets are locked up until you can afford to begin paying yourself an owner's distribution. But if you borrowed 80% of the startup costs instead, you would be in a much stronger financial position, having $400,000 in cash reserves put away in case you need it.

Be an Owner, Not a Lender

From the moment we get our first checking account, we are taught that saving our money in the bank is the safest, smartest thing you can possibly do with it. However, the super-rich understand that the returns that come along with owning appreciable assets dwarf the returns that come from lending the bank your money long-term.

The bank will certainly pay you some modest amount of interest for placing your trust in them and lending them your money for years to come. But then, they'll immediately turn around and make a loan to someone else with *your money*, with much more favorable terms to the bank than what they're paying you. So, in that instance, you are a lender. I'd rather you be an owner.

You can either lend the bank your money by leaving it on deposit or you can invest it into assets with growth and/or income potential, such as real estate or a small business.

Owning income-generating assets means you won't have to work as hard in the future.

Amazon is a great example of this. As a company, Amazon doesn't have to work as hard as it used to in order to make a profit. For decades, during its founder Jeff Bezos's tenure, Amazon famously purchased shares of a number of both public and private companies that still sit on their balance sheet today, such as Workday, Nextdoor, Juno Therapeutics, and several more. And as those companies grow and have success, it takes stress and pressure off of Amazon to turn a profit each quarter. That's what owning assets with long-term appreciation potential can do for you as well.

As you're building this portfolio, your income will be made up of a combination of active and passive sources. That combination will continually tilt until, ultimately, one day, it's all passive.

Be in the habit of acquiring appreciable assets over time rather than lending the bank your money indefinitely for next to no benefit. That's how true wealth is built. And that's how you reach financial independence sooner than conventional wisdom says you're allowed to.

Get Comfortable with an Acceptable Level of Risk

The most important wealthy habit to learn is how to override the fear and doubt that all of us have that keeps most people on the 9-to-5 treadmill until 65 (or later).

In Ben Horowitz's book, *The Hard Thing About Hard Things*, he shares the story of a conversation that changed his life. He was a recent college grad, planning to go to law school, but was afraid that by preparing himself for a safe, predictable career, he was also setting himself up to be bored for the rest of his life. Howoritz shared this concern with his mentor, who quickly told him, "You're going to be dead a lot longer than you're going to be alive. You might as well take your shot while you can."

That's heavy when you really think about it. How many of the people who made major contributions to the success of this country have now been dead longer than they were alive? From the Founding Fathers Washington, Franklin, and Hamilton, to the pioneers of the Industrial Revolution Rockefeller, Vanderbilt, and Ford, to Civil Rights icons such as Malcolm X, Martin Luther King Jr, and John F. Kennedy... All have been dead longer than they were alive.

If everyone throughout history had avoided risk at all costs, none of the major moments that have shaped this country for the better would have ever happened. We all owe it to ourselves to take a shot and see what it's like to live a life that's truly our own before our brief time on this earth is up.

Whenever I'm faced with a decision that has the potential to blow up in my face but also has the potential for tremendous upside, I simply ask myself, "What's the point of tiptoeing through life just to show up at death perfectly intact?" When my time comes, I want to have tried so many things and taken so many shots that I show up at death worn out and ready to go. I don't want one of my last thoughts to be "Man, I really wish I would've..."

Wealthy people often become wealthy because they're comfortable with the idea of taking risks. This doesn't mean that they take foolish risks or don't think before they act... But they understand that sometimes, in order to get something you've never had, you have to do something you've never done. In fact, in many instances, if you find that you're consistently hitting 100% of your shots, it means you're not taking enough risks.

Develop Your Team of Experts

Typically, by the time a person makes it to the super-rich club, they have already assembled a solid team of financial experts they can call at the drop of a hat. They believe that having a dedicated team of specialists is crucial to building and maintaining wealth. I would even argue that having a team of experts in your corner who can point out potential opportunities and help you to avoid common pitfalls all but ensures you hit a higher percentage of the shots you are taking.

Wealthy people don't call a company's 800 number in their time of need and explain their situation to a complete stranger. There are departments staffed with relationship managers whose entire calendar revolves around just a few names on their roster. They already have the client's important documents and know the other specialists on their team, so whenever a need arises, the process of getting to a solution happens quickly and smoothly.

Once upon a time, working-class people had access to these kinds of relationships as well. The average person could walk into a bank, for instance, and the banker would reference their kids by name and inquire about their plans for the summer. They could call their insurance broker, stockbroker, or tax professional, and launch right into the topic at hand, as that person was already well aware of their backstory.

But, unsurprisingly, as companies have searched for ways to cut costs and improve their bottom lines, the job of a relationship manager has primarily been replaced with chatbots and call centers - leading to interactions with professionals that are more transactional in nature. Meanwhile, the top 1% of households have continued to enjoy all of the benefits that come along with being connected in this way.

For instance, it came out in 2012 that Mark Zuckerberg had refinanced the $6 million mortgage on his California home, at an interest rate of 1.05%. The press not only made a big deal out of the fact that a billionaire tech entrepreneur "needed" a mortgage in the first place, but also wanted to know how he qualified for a rate that was so much lower than the average homeowner's. But what the myriad news articles failed to grasp was that the bank believed it was in their best interest to lose money on this one loan, if it meant that they could become the Zuckerberg family's bank of choice for years in the future.

Well before you make it to the Forbes Billionaires List, it can be beneficial to develop your own team of realtors, bankers, accountants, investment professionals, mortgage brokers, insurance agents, and so on... It is important to interview any financial professionals with whom you are contemplating forming a long-term working relationship - the same way you would a potential romantic partner. For instance, having a dedicated tax preparer who you work with year after year, means that someone is intimately familiar with your financial situation and should be able to help you make informed decisions that optimize your tax position.

The ideal tax strategy is the one that lowers your tax bill permanently, not just this year. However, not all accountants practice proactive tax planning. To find a tax professional who is capable of helping you look down the road, rather than one who will simply prepare and submit your return each year, your interview process needs to reflect that ultimate desire. When meeting with this person, it is not only important that you have questions prepared to ask them, but also pay attention to whether they have any questions for you.

Similarly, if you are seeking out the services of a financial planner, it is not enough to simply ask them about their service offering. Ask them how they manage their own money, and be careful to listen to whether their answer aligns with your own investment philosophy and what you're looking for. For instance, if you like to trade options, you may find that an investment advisor who believes in only owning passive index funds is not capable of providing the type of guidance you're looking for.

Ask them what types of clients they typically work with, and how many of them are in a similar position as you. Ask them whether they specialize in any particular domain within their field. Ask them how often you can expect to hear from them, and whether you will be billed separately for each conversation. These are the types of questions that go beyond determining whether they are qualified, and instead focus on whether they are the best fit for *you*.

Don't simply base your search on whichever professional is charging the lowest fee. Look for someone who has expertise in all of the areas that matter to you. For example, if you own multiple rental properties (or expect to soon), a tax preparer who specializes in working with real estate investors is most likely to help you save the most in taxes. However, an accountant with that type of specialized expertise is unlikely to also be the lowest cost option.

CHAPTER 8

USE THE TAX CODE TO YOUR ADVANTAGE

One of the most impactful things you can do for yourself on your way to financial independence is to not only gain a solid understanding of your own personal tax situation but also to do everything you can to (legally) pay as little in taxes each year as possible.

Too often, people will focus all of their attention and effort on growing their income and getting into the right investments at the right time, with little to no regard for how much of those gains they are on track to give back in the form of taxes. But, what good does it do you to spend hours on end researching the perfect stock, for example, just to end up giving back most of your gains due to selling too soon and paying the highest tax rate on your earnings?

A relentless focus on minimizing your tax bill will likely do more for you on the road to financial independence than trying to squeeze out the next 2% of return on an investment or negotiating with your boss for an additional $5,000 of salary.

We are taught that paying taxes is just as natural a part of life as breathing, eating, or dying. Some politicians would even tell you it's your patriotic duty to fork over 20, 30, maybe even 50% of your hard-earned dollars every year for the good of the republic. The reality is that the super-rich do not pay anything more in taxes each year than they absolutely have to.

Understanding your tax situation goes beyond knowing how much you will owe or receive as a refund every year. It's about understanding how all of the pieces on the board interact with each other and which levers you can pull to help create your desired outcome.

The U.S. was founded on a rebellion by the wealthy against taxes imposed by the British. It's in the very fabric of our DNA to have an aversion to taxes.

The Working Class Pay Taxes First, While the Wealthy Pay Taxes Last

There's a formula related to paying income taxes that the working class often gets wrong. That is, they follow this pattern: earn income, pay taxes, then spend whatever is left over. However, the super-rich take a different approach. They earn, spend, and then pay taxes on what's left over.

That's because the super-rich focus primarily on the assets column of their balance sheet, while the working class focuses on their income statement. This is why the working class gives away a third of their income every year to the tax man. Said another way, you'd have to work all the way through April to pay the government before making anything for yourself. That's four whole months of your life traded away to satisfy your tab with the government.

This is primarily due to the significant difference between active income and passive income. According to the Tax Code, a passive activity is any venture in which the taxpayer does not materially participate. Whether through business ownership or investments, as long as you are able to stay out of the day-to-day operations, there are some tax advantages to generating at least a portion of your income this way.

Active income, however, is synonymous with earned income. It refers to income received from performing a service, including wages, salaries, and tips, and is subject to ordinary income tax rates. Depending on a taxpayer's gross income amount, the rates applied to ordinary income can be significantly higher than the rates on any other type of income.

Considering it's only the wealthiest people and corporations who have the resources to lobby Congress to make the changes they want to see, the tax code is essentially written by wealthy people for wealthy people. However, by extension, it also benefits those of us who have the wherewithal to leverage the tax code and use it to our advantage as well.

For example, it was wealthy Texas oilmen who lobbied Congress to create the Roth IRA to allow them to pass along retirement assets to their children tax-free. But now, we can all reap the benefits of this type of account, even if we aren't nearly as wealthy as the people it was originally created for.

Contrary to popular opinion, the tax code is not necessarily written to advantage any singular wealthy person over anyone else. Instead, I believe the government uses the tax code to incentivize the kinds of behaviors it would like to see in the broader economy.

For instance, a healthy economy is one where everyone who wants a job has a job. Yet, the federal government does not want to be responsible for employing every working-age American. Thus, the government prefers for entrepreneurs to start small businesses, grow them, and continuously hire more workers. And the tax code incentivizes them to do so.

Another great example is housing. The government would like for every family in America to have a quality, affordable place to live. However, it does not want to be in the business of building and managing real estate for its citizens. Thus, the tax code incentivizes real estate developers and investors to do the work instead.

The government's preference for such behaviors is evidenced by its treatment of income generated through investments in both real estate and small businesses. In both cases, as long as the investment is held for more than 12 months and one day, income earned is taxed at the much more attractive long-term capital gains rate.

The tax code also incentivizes passive income over active income. And since wealthier people tend to earn a majority of their income from passive activities, it's yet another reason why the super-rich typically pay a smaller percentage of their income in taxes. The government rewards you for being financially independent and owning income-generating assets that are beneficial to society.

As I mentioned, it's through the tax code that the government incentivizes certain behaviors, so there are deductions that come along with being a business owner. Almost every expense you'll have as a self-employed person or business owner is deductible as long as it was used to do something ordinary and useful in the course of running that business.

While you should, by all means, take advantage of these deductions if you are entitled to them, be wary of advice given out on platforms such as YouTube and TikTok telling you that all you have to do is register a business and rack up expenses to save on income taxes. If the IRS were to ever decide that your business venture lacked legitimacy, and instead deemed it a hobby, not only would all of the losses you reported be disallowed, but the IRS would assess significant penalties and fines as well.

The IRS may be slow, but it's not stupid. They have computers crawling through tax returns and pattern matching to catch these sorts of irregularities. It might take them a few years to finally get to you, but eventually, they catch on.

Understand How the Next Dollar Earned Will Impact Your Tax Bill

The tax code is written in pencil, not in ink. It is important to pay attention to major pieces of tax legislation as they are announced each year to be sure whether and how they will impact you. The income tax rates are adjusted annually for inflation, as well as the limits on certain deductions and contributions to retirement plans and other types of workplace benefits.

Each time a new administration comes to power, they likely bring with them an overhaul to the previous regime's tax policies.

In the United States, we live within a progressive tax system whereby tax rates are typically divided into income brackets, with each bracket corresponding to a specific range of income. That means that the rate of taxation the IRS imposes increases as your personal income rises.

At the time of this writing, the marginal tax rates for ordinary income include 10%, 12%, 22%, 24%, 32%, 35%, and 37%. These rates are applied to income in a series of steps, otherwise known as a progressive tax. The first portion of income is taxed at 10%, the next portion is taxed at 12%, the next at 22%, and so on. As individuals move into higher income brackets, the applicable tax rate for that portion of their income increases.

The total amount of tax you are responsible for each year is actually a blend of these rates and is referred to as your effective tax rate. In other words, when you say you're in the 35% tax bracket, that doesn't mean you'll actually pay 35% on every dollar you earn. It is just as important to pay attention to your effective tax rate as you would your marginal tax rate when making decisions related to your income taxes.

The Tax Code is Most Generous to Those Who Own Real Estate

Real estate is the absolute best asset you can own as an investor. That is because the U.S. tax code contains numerous provisions that favor individuals and entities who choose to invest in real estate. As I said previously, the U.S. Government recognizes the significant role real estate plays, not only in the growth of the economy but in the development of local communities as well. So, the tax code is written to encourage investment and development within the real estate sector.

For instance, if an individual owns a home as their primary residence, their ability to deduct the interest they pay on their mortgage each year is dependent on whether they itemize or take the standard deduction. However, real estate investors are allowed to deduct the interest paid on mortgage debt from their rental income, whether they take the standard deduction or not. The same goes for any property taxes paid each year.

Real estate investors are also permitted to take a deduction for depreciation, which is a non-cash deduction that allows a property's owner to recover the cost of acquiring the property over its useful life. According to the IRS, an investment property's useful life is exactly 27.5 years - meaning that each year, an investor is allowed to write off 3.6% of the home's purchase price. By deducting a portion of the property's cost each year, investors get to shield a significant portion of their rental income from taxes, thereby improving cash flow.

The one downside to the depreciation deduction is that you must proportionally reduce your cost basis in that property simultaneously. If you were to sell the property at any point, you would be forced to pay back the deductions you enjoyed each year. But, don't worry. The Tax Code has an answer for that, too. Section 1031 of the Internal Revenue Code allows investors to defer capital gains taxes when they sell a property, as long as they reinvest the proceeds into another property of greater value.

This provision helps investors to defer paying taxes until a final sale is made - presumably decades later, if ever. Similar to the "buy, borrow, and die" strategy, as a real estate investor, you may carry your gains forward forever by rolling them into the next property again and again. And once you pass away, your heirs would be permitted to restart their cost basis on the date they inherited the property. Thus, it is possible to (figuratively) take those capital gains with you to your grave.

A Good Tax Accountant is Worth Every Penny

Every year, somewhere between January 1st and April 15th, millions of Americans work their way through the five stages of grief as they prepare and file their tax returns.

In general, there are two options available to help taxpayers complete and submit their annual tax return. On the one hand, there is the option to prepare and file your return yourself. On the other hand, there is the option to hire a professional to do all the work for you instead.

While there are several software tools designed to help make that process easier, filing your own taxes often requires hours of locating, sorting through, and preparing documents, checking and re-checking your math, and maybe a few intense Google searches.

In the end, you still can end up missing a key item or two that makes all the difference in you owing the government or them owing you. If you underpaid, that means you will end up paying the government to cover any taxes due as well as any applicable penalties for late-or-under-payment. However, if you overpaid and are due a refund, it is also not an ideal situation because you could have kept that money throughout the year and either saved or invested it rather than allowing the government to hold onto it as an interest-free loan.

Tax preparation software can often be a great alternative to hiring a tax professional and is sometimes the better choice. For those who have a straightforward tax situation with only one or two income sources and few deductions, basic tax preparation software services are created with you in mind.

Generally, when someone chooses to self-prepare their taxes rather than hire a professional, it is in the interest of saving a few dollars in associated fees. However, in addition to simply filling on your behalf, a professional preparer can answer questions, research the tax code, and help you navigate complex issues that may be unique to your personal situation.

When you make the decision to hire a tax professional, be sure that you choose one who has a level of experience and specialization that suits your needs. Some accountants are general practitioners, whereas others specialize in working with small businesses, non-profits, or expats living overseas.

The two most popular professional credentials for tax professionals are Certified Public Accountants (CPAs) and Enrolled Agents (EAs). The IRS holds CPAs and EAs to a high standard and often audits professionally prepared returns less frequently.

CPAs are considered the gold standard when it comes to tax preparation. They are licensed accounting professionals who typically possess a graduate degree in accounting, have studied for and passed the rigorous CPA exam, and have achieved significant experience in the field. While CPAs are trained in a variety of accounting procedures, such as audits and preparing complex financial documents, some of them will also perform tax preparation tasks.

In contrast, EAs are trained specifically in the laws and procedures that govern tax preparation. For this reason, EAs tend to be the less costly option of the two. They may also represent you in front of the IRS in case of an audit or simply serve as your personal representative in the event that the IRS has any clarifying questions regarding your return.

Smart tax experts and accountants are worth what they charge. It's less about how much they cost you and more about how much they save you in the long run. In fact, a good tax accountant can be far cheaper than overpaying the government due to an error.

CHAPTER 9

HOW TO INVEST

One simple tenant of the American Dream is that each generation should be more economically prosperous than the generation that came before it. Not less.

And the uncomfortable truth is that Gen X-ers, Millennials, and Gen Zers alike don't see themselves as any better off than their parents' generations. In 1980, people under the age of 40 controlled 19% of the aggregate wealth in the United States. But in 2020, that number sat at just 9%. Clearly, we're moving in the wrong direction.

Not all Americans own investments. And many of those that do only get exposure to the stock market through their workplace retirement plan such as a 401(k), 403(b), etc. In fact, according to recent reports, about 70% of all stocks available for trading are owned by only 10% of investors.

Part of the reason for this lack of exposure is the historical barriers to entry that have kept marginalized people from enjoying the same opportunities and access as their white male peers. However, with the amount of information now widely available to all would-be investors, as well as the democratization of stock trading thanks to online brokerages and mobile apps, I'd argue that the second biggest culprit keeping people on the sidelines is *fear*.

For more than a couple of centuries, the most powerful long-term wealth generator in this country has been property ownership. And right after that, the next best way to get rich has been to invest in the US stock market.

But the way that you invest for a traditional retirement is not the same way you'd invest if it's your goal to reach financial independence in your 30s, 40s, or 50s. More on this later.

There is Such a Thing as Having Too Much Cash

It's important that before you invest, you build an emergency fund capable of covering three months of expenses (if you're married) and six months of expenses (if you're single). This savings account will act as your insurance policy against any meaningful stoppage in your income, and should not be used for any other purpose. Once you've built up your emergency reserves, focus on paying off any unproductive debts.

There are certainly those who argue that a person might need more than three to six months to secure a new job if they were to lose one. While I won't argue with the need to feel like your backside is absolutely covered, I do believe that holding anything beyond a year's worth of expenses in cash is a missed opportunity.

When cash sits in a bank account, it loses value over time - due to the silent thief, otherwise known as inflation. To make matters worse, those dollars sitting at the bank don't earn nearly the rate of return they would if they were invested.

Consider that since its inception in the 1950s, the S&P 500 index has returned an average of 10% to investors each year. Thus, the gap between what your cash earns when it's parked in your bank account and 10% is your opportunity cost.

As the renowned investor Warren Buffett famously says, "you should be greedy when others are fearful and be fearful when others are greedy". You don't even need to be invested in the most speculative assets to earn a respectable return. Just be honest with yourself about your willingness to take on additional risk in exchange for higher potential investment returns, and develop your investing strategy based on that.

It can be scary to consider parting with your hard-earned cash in exchange for the unknown. But if you desire to reach financial independence before your 80th birthday, then simply socking away all of your savings into an account at the bank is not going to cut it. It cannot be overstated just how powerful a force compounding is, and there is no greater source for growing your liquid savings over the long term than the stock market.

To be clear, I am not advocating for leaving the safety of cash to go speculating. At its core, investing is about putting your money to work in such a way that you expect it to grow more over time than it would if you were to simply park it in some sort of risk-free account, such as a high-yield savings account or treasury bond.

You expect that years down the road, those dollars will have compounded on top of themselves and will return you significantly more than the risk-free rate of return that you passed up, as well as outperform the average inflation rate for that same period.

Speculation, however, is more akin to gambling. If you were to walk into a casino this evening and plop down $500 on the blackjack table, you would assume that your chances of going home with less than $500 at the end of the night are much greater than the chances of leaving there a winner. But it's the ridiculously low odds that make gambling so appealing.

Your intention makes all of the difference. Though "investing" and "speculating" are two terms that are often conflated together, their respective actions have two very different intentions and can create two distinctly different outcomes.

Build Your Core Portfolio

Now that you've paid off unproductive debt and built your cash savings, it's time to put your dollars to work in the public stock markets. But rather than buying a bunch of individual stocks right out of the gate that could move left, right, or center on any given day, you want to first invest 50% of your investible dollars in an index fund that captures the broader market and is meant to grow longer term.

An exchange-traded fund (ETF), such as the SPY, is designed to capture the performance of the S&P 500 Index, offering investors exposure to 500 of the largest U.S. companies across various industries in a single investment. Similarly, a mutual fund such as Vanguard Total Stock Market, which owns approximately 3,750 stocks, aims to mirror the performance of the entire U.S. stock market, providing investors comprehensive exposure to small, mid, and large-cap stocks. Either of these would make a great starting point and would help you gain broad exposure before adding on more specialized investments.

Once you've allocated 50% to your index fund of choice, you can add in some individual stocks that you're interested in. But make sure these stocks are ones in industries that you understand and are willing to keep up with. For example, if you follow fashion and enjoy keeping up with trends, you'd want to first add a few well-known designers and retailers to your portfolio. Or, if you work in cybersecurity, it's a good idea to invest in cybersecurity stocks first because you'll understand the lingo and the earnings guidance the companies are putting out each quarter.

This familiarity will allow you to get comfortable with the markets and gain a better understanding of why and when prices move the way they do. Rather than buying stocks with the intention to sell them in a few days and catch a wave, invest in companies that you can reasonably expect will perform well over the long term.

Develop the criteria you will use to determine when to buy a stock *and* when to sell it. What's your offramp? It's important to set a target for exiting an investment before buying into it. Write it down. And commit to it. This will help you separate your emotions from the investing process.

One of the questions I always ask myself before hitting the "buy" button is, "Am I going to regret not owning this stock in three years?" If the answer is not a resounding "yes," then I don't feel like I have to pull the trigger and buy this stock right away. This logic also works the other way. If it's a stock I already own and I'm trying to decide whether it's time to sell, if I won't regret not owning it three years from now, then I am okay letting it go, considering my personal time horizon for buying an individual stock is at least three years.

It's important not to get carried away when making your shopping list. Rather than adding a new ticker symbol to your portfolio every time you hear about a new company that's working on something exciting, limit yourself to no more than 30 individual stocks in your portfolio at one time. Any more than that will be too difficult to keep track of in the midst of everything else happening in your life.

As you continue to add additional money into your brokerage account, follow the pattern of adding half to your index fund, and with the remainder, buy a few more shares of your favorite stocks - preferably your best performers. When markets are performing well, our natural inclination is to sell our winners, take the gains so that we can brag about how well we're doing, and hang on to our losers to give them time to recover. But history has taught us we should do the opposite.

Imagine if you applied this logic to sports... In the 90s, when the Chicago Bulls were racking up trophy after trophy, no one in their right mind watched Michael Jordan lead his team to the finals for the fourth, fifth, or sixth time and thought, "I bet this will be the year that MJ lets us down." Absolutely not! And why?... Because winners win.

The most impactful things you can do as an investor are also some of the most counterintuitive things you can do as an investor. Dollar-cost averaging and rebalancing are other great examples of this.

It's important to remember that the way you lose a dollar is not necessarily the same way you have to earn a dollar back. Said another way, just because you lose $1,000 in a bad investment in the stock market does not necessitate that you earn it back the same way.

Money is fungible. If you earn an additional $1,000 by doing something completely different, you still end out in the same place. So don't get so focused on chasing after your losses that you just end up throwing good money after bad. It's often better to simply cut your losses and move on.

Keep it Simple!

Investing should not be about making big bets and following the crowd. You should instead seek to simplify your investment philosophy as much as possible and get clear on what you own and why you own it.

Rule #1 of investing is to only invest in things you truly understand. It's critical to understand how an asset could perform through different market conditions. You should have an understanding of what type of market conditions that particular investment will flourish under and what would make it crater. You should also have a clear understanding of whether that investment introduces more or less risk into your portfolio than average, and why that is.

While it is true that investing carries some risks, the reality is that the majority of people who lose their shirts in the stock market are guilty of both "investing" in something they didn't actually understand *and* putting more money at risk than they could afford to lose.

Beware of get-rich-quick schemes and straight-up scams. In a mania, buried underneath the surface, is all of the junk that people wealthier than you have been holding onto, just waiting for a moment such as this one to unload it onto unsuspecting investors.

Think about the SPAC craze we just witnessed throughout the COVID era. Many of the companies that came onto the exchanges using this non-traditional means of public offering have given back 70, 80, or even 90% of their value since then. This means that the wealthy investors in the company who cashed out on IPO day made their money back simply by transferring stock in that worthless company over to you.

In a mania where small-dollar penny stocks once left for dead are suddenly en vogue, this is where it's time to heed the words of Mr. Buffett and be fearful. As my mom used to say to me as the young, money-obsessed child that I was, "Just as hard as you are working to learn how to make your money, there is someone else out there working even harder to learn how to take it from you." Those words couldn't be truer today.

There's a growing number of investment products being pushed on younger, high-earning investors because they are typically more risk-tolerant and unassuming. These "products," such as alt-coins, NFTs, staking rewards, etc. are often marketed under the guise of an alternative investment.

That's a blanket jargony industry term that basically means the investment is not a traditional stock or bond and should perform differently from those two, especially during extreme market conditions. You want alternatives in your portfolio because they're not correlated to stocks or bonds, and should help shield you from big market downswings whenever they occur. But all that glitters is not a true alternative investment. Sometimes, it's just fool's gold.

Plan Your Work. Work Your Plan

Many people think the way to start investing is to jump in and buy the hot stock that everyone's been talking about. But there's a more strategic and thoughtful way to get started, and it starts with defining the reason you're investing these specific dollars at this moment.

You can think about your different investment accounts as different buckets that are going to serve different purposes over time. Before you get sucked into the latest trendy investment, get clear on your goal for this particular bucket.

Are these funds that you are putting to work simply to watch them grow? Is it your hope that putting these dollars to the side now will allow them to grow and subsequently multiply your buying power decades down the road? Have you decided you'd like to make a big purchase in a couple years and want to make sure that this money doesn't get eaten up by inflation in the meantime?

Each of these scenarios carries with it a different investing approach. For example, if you want to buy a house next year, your investment has less than a 12-month time horizon, which means that you're not able to take on much risk at all. You can't afford to take the chance that what you've put away toward that purchase will be worth significantly less when it's time to go to the closing table.

But if you're saving for your retirement in twenty-five years, you have a much longer time horizon and can be more aggressive in your approach. Since you'd have multiple market cycles to recover any losses you might experience along the way, you can afford a higher level of risk in that particular portfolio.

When you've clearly defined why you're investing this money and how much time you have to achieve that goal, you can calculate the amount of return you need to receive each year, which will also help to determine what to invest in. Reflecting on this first allows you to block out the noise from your friends and neighbors whenever they brag to you about the investments they're making and the returns they're (allegedly) receiving.

Embrace Investments Outside the Stock Market

Once you've built a substantial portfolio in the public stock markets, you should seek out investment opportunities in the private markets as well. According to Blackstone Global Investment Firm, 85% of companies that generate $250,000,000 or more in revenue each year are private, which means only 15% are available to investors in the public markets.

People tend to think of this as investing in the coder in the hoodie, working to invent the next Facebook. But in reality, it could be as simple as investing in a friend who's a physician looking to go into private practice.

In my experience, it is possible to save your way to a net worth between $2-3 million by your mid-sixties through diligent saving, avoiding conspicuous consumption, and investing in the stock market. Through the powers of compounding and dollar cost averaging, you can certainly retire a millionaire.

However, for those who wish to become financially independent in their 30s, 40s, or 50s, it is imperative that you begin investing outside of the stock market as soon as practicable because you will likely need a much larger nest egg. In my day job, the two most common ways that I see people managing to amass a 7 or 8-figure net worth is either through long-term appreciation in real estate, or by being closely attached to a high-growth business - whether as founder/CEO, a key first hire, or an early investor.

It's important to keep some of your net worth in the public markets so that if something happens tomorrow, you have access to liquidity and can convert those investments to cash in just a couple days. However, $2 million is probably the maximum amount that most people need to have invested in the public markets at any given time.

Beyond that $2 million mark, those dollars are likely better off invested in private equity, private real estate, or venture capital, as that's where consistent double-digit returns tend to come from. To be sure, investing in the private markets is often riskier because the assets are a lot less liquid, but they typically come with better returns as well.

If You Choose to Invest in Real Estate, Focus on Cash Flow

Owning real estate has long been the cornerstone of wealth creation in the United States. And for those pursuing financial independence, it can be a great idea to build a portfolio of rental properties that generate income and will one day pay you to stay in bed.

However, it does not happen overnight, and what online influencers and message boards often neglect to mention is the actual amount of time and energy required to manage a property. From screening tenants to collecting rent, performing maintenance, and managing online listings, the demands of owning real estate are a significant undertaking.

Realistically, building a sustainable, income-generating real estate portfolio takes work. While you may be able to outsource most tasks related to owning and maintaining a property, it is important to keep in mind that every dollar spent takes you further from the ultimate goal: reaching cash flow positivity.

This is the point where the total income from the property exceeds all associated expenses. It is a critical milestone for investors, marking the transition from a monthly expense to a profitable endeavor. Achieving cash flow positivity is a key indicator of a successful real estate investment, as it demonstrates the property's ability to generate sustainable, passive income beyond the costs of maintaining and managing it.

Passive real estate investing *should* require minimal active involvement, allowing investors to reap the benefits of ownership without daily management responsibilities. As such, it can neither be overstated how critical it is to choose the right property manager nor how important it is to replace them the moment it becomes clear they are no longer the right fit. Mismanagement can quickly turn what would be a passive investment into an active money pit.

Another key cornerstone of passive real estate investing is to always have a clear exit strategy. Whether your plan is to invest in a turnkey property that is rental-ready, a quick flip, or a long-term hold for generational wealth transfer, knowing your exit plan can guide better decision-making and protect your returns. Too often, overly optimistic investors make the leap and purchase property before determining how and when they expect to turn a profit.

CONCLUSION

REMEMBER WHY YOU'RE HERE

As we reach the end of this book, I want you to take a moment to reflect on why the journey to financial independence matters to you. What is driving you to seek such control over the way you spend your time? What answers were you searching for when you picked up this book?

Maybe you want to have more control over your time so you can be present for your kids.

Maybe the 9-to-5 grind has drained your creativity and passion, and you want to reclaim that part of yourself.

Maybe you grew up watching your parents struggle with money, and you want to build a better future for yourself.

Maybe you have unconventional dreams and goals that a 9-to-5 would stand in the way of.

Maybe you have a charity or social cause that you want to dedicate your time and energy to.

Maybe you've had a similar thought to the one I had when I saw that billboard back in 2018: I don't want to spend so much time working that my wife and kids only remember the times that I *wasn't* there.

Maybe you, like many people born after the baby boom generation, are asking, "Who says that I have to wait until I'm a senior citizen to live life on my terms?"

Whatever your reasons are, hold tightly to them as you begin this journey toward financial independence. At times, it can feel like it's taking too long to get there, or like you aren't making much progress. In those moments, remember why this journey matters to you. Nothing worth having comes easy.

What I have proposed in this book—designing and following a road map to financial independence—is not a quick-fix solution. And that's the beauty of it. Quick fixes aren't sustainable. They don't work.

But the journey to financial independence, as I have laid it out here, only requires you to think creatively, stay disciplined, and have a bias toward action. Thus, financial independence can be attained by anyone who wants it badly enough.

Throughout this book, I've shared with you some of the very same principles that have helped others to build a financially independent future. Now, it's time to get to work and apply them.

Remember, it won't happen for you simply because you read this book from cover to cover. The real work is just beginning. However, by taking small steps, adopting new habits, and thinking differently, you can and will reach your financial independence point.

Beware the naysayers. To most people you know, these ideas will sound crazy. They've never even considered that it might be possible to buy themselves more time for the people and things they love. They may even give you compelling-sounding reasons why *you* can't do it either.

Just be careful with whom you choose to share the details of your plan... To most people, financial independence is unattainable and not even worth pursuing. This is where your tribe will come in handy. Having a few people you can call on every now and then, especially when you feel discouraged, will help to drown out any negative self-talk trying to creep in.

Keep in mind that there are countless examples of people who started out right where you are, created a vision of a better life, and pursued it unapologetically. They didn't let the limiting beliefs of others stop them from designing a life that was truly their own.

Imagine how great it will feel to wake up every morning and make an active choice of how to spend your time each day—focused on what you *want* to do, not what you *have* to do.

This is the life that I wish for you. It only requires that you take that first step. The rest of the staircase will reveal itself in due time.

NEXT STEPS

Thank you for reading! It's been an absolute joy to share these insights and strategies with you, and I'm thrilled at the thought of you applying them on your path to financial independence. Along the way, we would love to be your cheerleaders, so be sure to reach out and let us know how you're doing. Your successes, big and small, are what we're here for.

Malcolm Ethridge
hello@malcolmethridge.com
www.malcolmethridge.com

As you embark on your journey toward financial independence, you might find yourself in need of a little push. That's what we're here for. By scanning the QR code below or visiting the link, you may schedule a complimentary consultation with Malcolm and his team to receive expert help in crafting your own financial independence roadmap.

www.malcolmethridge.com/services

MEET MALCOLM

Malcolm Ethridge is a Certified Financial Planner (CFP®), speaker, blogger, podcast host, and self-proclaimed personal finance nerd. He is also an on-air contributor at CNBC, where he dissects the market news of the day and offers insights into corporate earnings reports and major announcements.

In his day job, Malcolm leads a team creating customized financial plans, designed to help senior managers and executives in tech make sense of some of the most complex financial situations that working professionals tend to face. His areas of expertise include retirement planning, investment portfolio development, tax planning, equity compensation, and other executive benefits.

Made in United States
North Haven, CT
20 April 2024